LUCKY SCIENCE

LUCKY SCIENCE

Accidental Discoveries from Gravity to Velcro, with Experiments

Royston M. Roberts
Jeanie Roberts

John Wiley & Sons, Inc.

New York • Chichester • Brisbane • Toronto • Singapore

This text is printed on acid-free paper.

Illustrated by Laurel Aiello.

The publisher and the authors have made every reasonable effort to insure that the experiments and activities in this book are safe when conducted as instructed but assume no responsibility for any damage caused or sustained while performing the experiments or activities in this book. Parents, guardians, and/or teachers should supervise young readers who undertake the experiments and activities in this book.

Library of Congress Cataloging-in-Publication Data
Roberts, Royston M.
    Lucky science: accidental discoveries from gravity to velcro,
with experiments / Royston Roberts and Jeanie Roberts.
        p.   cm.
    Includes index.
    ISBN 0-471-00954-7 (acid-free paper)
    Q172.5.S47R62   1995
    500—dc20   94-10373

Printed in the United States of America
10 9 8 7 6 5 4 3 2

TRADEMARKS AND PATENTS

Dedicated to
  the youth of today
  who may become
  the scientists of tomorrow

CONTENTS

Contents

INTRODUCTION

What do Velcro™, penicillin, Teflon™, and the Dead Sea Scrolls have in common? They were all discovered by accident, or **serendipity**, as were hundreds of other things that make everyday living more pleasant, healthy, or interesting. Since these accidental discoveries are of scientific things, we can call them "Lucky Science."

The word *serendipity* was made up by the Englishman Horace Walpole in 1754. Walpole had read a fairy story about the adventures of "The Three Princes of Serendip." (Serendip is an old name for the island country near India now known as Sri Lanka.) The Princes of Serendip "were always making discoveries, by accidents and sagacity, of things which they were not in quest of." Walpole used the term *serendipity* to describe some of his own accidental discoveries.

Most of the people who have been blessed by serendipity do not mind admitting their good fortune. They know that serendipity is more than just luck. It also means that the person making the accidental discovery is smart enough to understand that the accident is showing him or her something new and important. This is what Horace Walpole meant by "discoveries by accidents and sagacity." **Sagacity** is another word for "intelligence." Louis Pasteur, who made important discoveries that you will read about in this book, expressed this idea well. He said, "In the fields of observation, chance favors only the prepared mind."

For each of the examples of serendipity described in this book, there are hundreds of others that were not included. Maybe you will have the good fortune to have one happen to you. We hope that this book will encourage you to develop your knowledge of science so that you will be prepared to take advantage of serendipity. At the end of each chapter in this book, we've included a short experiment to start you on your way.

If you have had serendipity in your own life, or if you know of others who have, please bring these stories to our attention so that we can include them in future editions of this book.

And there should be future editions, because serendipity is something that happens every day, or at least *accidents* do, and it is up to you to turn them into discoveries!

THE EUREKA MAN

Archimedes Measures Volume

Archimedes, the Greek mathematician, lived in Syracuse, Greece, in the third century B.C. He is famous for inventing the lever, the "Archimedes screw" (which is still used in Egypt to raise the waters of the Nile for irrigation), and the law of hydrostatics. But we won't go into these now, because he is probably most famous for running naked from the public baths through the streets of Syracuse shouting "Eureka, eureka!" (which means "I've found it, I've found it!").

What had Archimedes found? What so excited him that he forgot to put on his clothes before dashing home? To answer this question we need to know what Archimedes had on his mind as he stepped into the baths that day.

Hiero, the king of Syracuse, had asked a goldsmith to make a crown for him from pure gold. But when he got the finished crown, the king had doubts about whether the goldsmith had put all the gold into it. Couldn't the goldsmith have substituted a less valuable metal, such as silver or copper, for some of the gold and kept the gold that was not used?

When gold is mixed with other metals it keeps its rich gold color even when large amounts of the other metals are added. Pure gold is called 24-carat gold. The metal commonly used for jewelry, 14-carat gold, is 58 percent gold and 42 percent another metal, often silver or copper. This mixture is used because it is stronger and will wear better than pure gold, and it looks almost exactly like pure gold.

King Hiero called in his friend Archimedes and presented the famous mathematician with the job of finding out if the crown was indeed pure gold. Archimedes was a very clever mathematician and engineer. He realized that if he could determine the **volume** of Hiero's crown (that is, how much space was occupied by the crown) he would be able to tell whether the crown was made of pure gold or of a mixture of gold with other metals. Archimedes knew that different materials having the same weight may have very different volumes.

When he saw water run over the top of the tub as he stepped into it, he realized that the volume of the overflow water (the water that was "displaced" by his body) was exactly equal to the volume of the part of his body that he had placed in the water. Now he saw a way of calculating the volume of any solid object, whether it was his foot or a crown. If he put the crown into a container filled to the brim with water, he could measure the volume of the displaced water and this would be equal to the volume of the crown.

Suppose Hiero had given the goldsmith a cube of pure gold that weighed exactly 5 pounds (2.27 kg). The edges of such a cube would measure 1.9 inches (4.9 cm) and the volume of the cube would be 7.19 cubic inches (118 cubic cm). If the goldsmith made the crown with *all* of this gold and *no other metal*, the crown would weigh the same, and the volume would be the same as that of the original cube, 7.19 cubic inches (118 cubic cm), although in a very different shape. If the goldsmith made the crown with only *half* of the pure gold and *an equal weight* of silver, the crown would weigh the same, but its volume would be larger, because an equal weight of silver would take up almost twice as much space as gold.

After Archimedes made his accidental discovery at the public baths, he measured the volume of Hiero's new crown by placing it in water and measuring the volume of the displaced water. When the king found out that the volume was considerably greater than it should have been for a crown made of pure gold, the dishonest goldsmith was executed. What was a fortunate discovery for Archimedes (serendipity!) was not so fortunate for the goldsmith.

So this accidental discovery of a way to measure the volume of any solid object was the cause of the excitement that led Archimedes to dash out of the bath unaware that he had left his clothes behind, shouting "Eureka!" as he went.

crown made of
pure gold
(volume = 118 cc)

crown made of
50% gold/50% silver
(volume = 167 cc)

The approximate difference in size between a solid gold crown weighing 5 pounds (2.27 kg) and a 50 percent gold/50 percent silver crown weighing 5 pounds (2.27 kg).

HOW YOU CAN ...

Measure the Volume of Common Objects

What you need ...

2 measuring bowls: a 1-quart (32 liq. oz) or 1-liter size and a ½-pint (8 liq. oz) or ¼-liter size

baking dish, approximately 13 × 9 × 2 inches (33.× 23 × 5 cm). A square or rectangular dish is best because it is easier to pour water out of a corner of it into a measuring bowl without spilling.

drinking glass or cup

tap water

kitchen tongs

any solid, irregularly shaped objects whose *volume* you wish to measure, for example, your hand, a tennis ball, or a piece of fruit

kitchen scale or balance [any type that will weigh 0.22 to 1 pound (100 to 454 g) accurately]

What you do ...

1. Fill the larger measuring bowl almost to the top with water. Place it in the middle of the baking dish and pour more water into it from a glass or cup until it is filled to the brim.

2. Carefully lower the object whose volume you wish to measure into the water in the bowl until the object is completely submerged. (You may have to use the tongs to do this successfully; for example, a banana will float.) The displaced water should run over the edge of the bowl and flow into the baking dish.

3. Lift the bowl out of the baking dish and empty the bowl.

4. Pour the water in the baking dish into the smaller measuring bowl and record the volume of the displaced water. This is also the volume of the object you placed in the water.

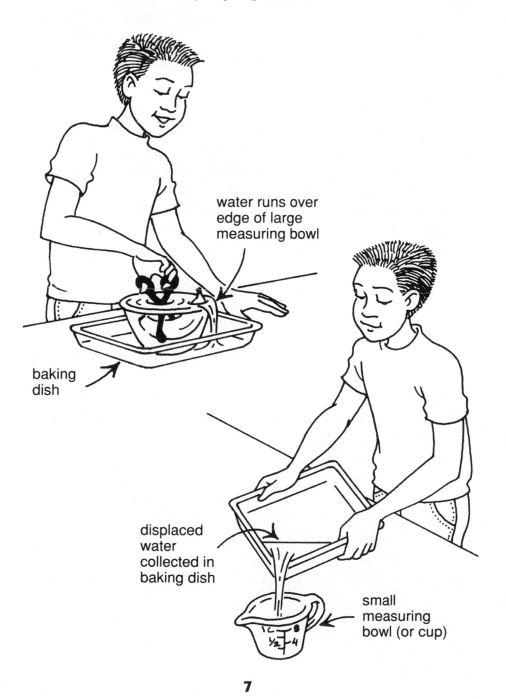

water runs over edge of large measuring bowl

baking dish

displaced water collected in baking dish

small measuring bowl (or cup)

Now try this ...

If you wish to compare the volumes of things that weigh the same, you can do the following: Take a baseball (the hardball type) and weigh it on a kitchen scale. Find some gravel or several small rocks and weigh them, choosing just enough pieces to weigh the same as the baseball. Now compare the volumes of the baseball and of the pieces of gravel or rocks that weigh the same.

What happened ...

When we did this experiment, we found the baseball weighed 5.4 ounces (150 g) and had a volume of 6.4 liquid ounces (190 cc). The gravel that weighed 5.4 ounces (150 g) had a volume of 1.7 liquid ounces (50 cc), only about one-third the volume of the baseball! This shows that gravel is three times as dense as the materials in a baseball. (**Density** is a measure of weight per unit of volume.)

AN APPLE FALLS

Sir Isaac Newton
Discovers Gravity

Everyone has heard the story of Sir Isaac Newton coming up with the theory of gravity when he saw an apple fall from a tree, but some people don't believe it really happened. We think that it did happen, and that this started him thinking about gravity and the many ways that gravity affects our world.

Sir Isaac Newton was born in England on Christmas Day in 1642. When Newton was a small boy he was sent away to a school about six miles from home, but when he was 14, his mother brought him home to run the farm. Newton was not happy being a farmer. He was more interested in mathematics and various mechanical hobbies. Fortunately, his uncle recognized Newton's potential and suggested that he be sent back to school to prepare for the university.

Newton entered Cambridge University in 1661 at the age of 18. During the next three years, he was able to study mathematics and science. While he was at Cambridge, the plague broke out in London, and the university was shut down to prevent further spread of the terrible disease. Newton returned home and spent two years learning on his own before returning to the university. It is during this time at home that we think Newton saw the famous apple drop. However, Newton did not write about the law of gravity until he published his famous book *Principia* about 20 years later.

One of Newton's friends, Dr. William Stukely, wrote about a talk he had with Newton when Newton was an old man. Stukely wrote that they were sitting under some apple trees after dinner, and Newton said that it reminded him of a time long ago when he watched an apple fall from a tree. Newton thought to himself, "Why should that apple always fall straight down to the ground? . . . Why should it not go sideways or upwards, but constantly to the earth's center?"

Of course, many people had seen an apple drop before, but Newton's prepared mind (from his studies at the university) helped him to figure out why the apple fell straight down to the ground instead of going "sideways or upwards." Before the apple fell, Newton had been thinking about the ways that two objects attract each other. When the apple fell straight down from the tree to the earth, he realized that the center of the earth must somehow attract the apple. This force of attraction he described as **gravity**.

This discovery also helped Newton understand why the moon stayed in its orbit around the earth. Another man writing about New-

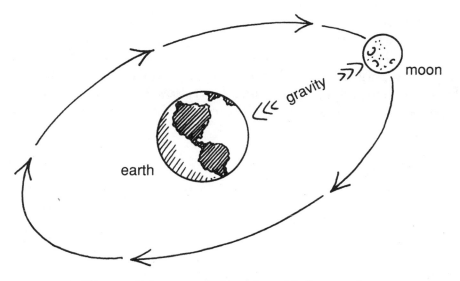

The earth's moon is kept in orbit by gravity.

ton said that "as in a vision, he saw that if the mysterious pull of the earth can act through space as far as the top of a tree, of a mountain, and even to a bird soaring high in the air, or to the clouds, so it might even reach so far as the moon." The earth's gravity pulls the moon toward it, but the moon is moving fast enough to keep circling the earth without falling toward it. In the same way, the spaceships orbiting the earth today use their rockets to make them go fast enough to keep them from falling back to earth. When they want to return to earth, they fire rockets from the front of the ship to slow them down. Then the force of gravity pulls the spaceship to earth.

Newton's law of gravity allows us to understand not only how the moon stays in its orbit, but also how our earth and the other planets revolve around the sun. We also understand how other planets revolve around other suns (stars) throughout the universe.

Gravity and Weight

The reason anything has weight is because of gravity. The gravity on the moon is much weaker than the gravity on earth, because the moon is much smaller than the earth. Because of this, a person would weigh much less on the moon than on the earth. We can stand, sit, and lie on the earth because of gravity, but astronauts are weightless in space, where gravity has little effect.

We use two basic types of scales to weigh things: the spring type and the balance type. The balance type is more accurate. This is the kind of scale you see in the doctor's office. You stand on the scale and move a weight across a numbered beam until the beam becomes balanced. The following experiment will show how a simple balance scale works and how it can be used to show how weight is related to gravity.

HOW YOU CAN ...

Demonstrate and Use Gravity

What you need ...

triangular file (available at hardware stores)

yardstick (meterstick)

2 pieces of strong string, each about 2 feet (60 cm) long

some things to balance against each other, such as a banana and an apple

2 or 3 heavy books

What you do ...

1. Using the file, make a small groove at the midpoint of the measuring stick. Make the groove *across* the stick, perpendicular to the long length of the stick.

2. Tie one end of one of the strings around the banana and make a loop at the other end of the string that will go over the measuring stick. Do the same thing with the apple and the other piece of string.

3. Place the file on top of a table so that it sticks out about 3 to 4 inches (8 to 10 cm) from the edge of the table. Put the heavy books on the end of the file that lies on the table to keep it in place. Place the measuring stick on the file with the groove in the middle positioned on the edge of the file, so that the stick balances.

4. Loop the string holding the banana over the end of the stick at the 8-inch (20-cm) position on the measuring stick, letting the banana hang down.

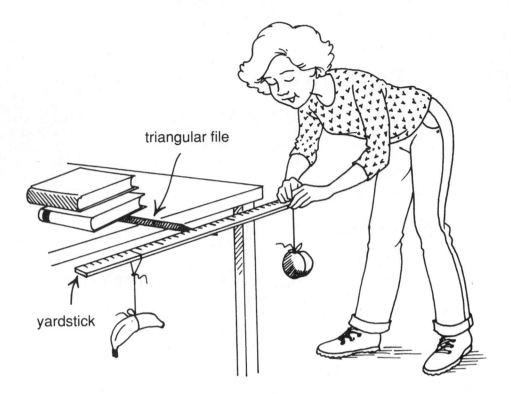

triangular file

yardstick

5. Next, hang the string holding the apple from a position on the measuring stick so that it just balances the banana. Note the inch (or centimeter) position of the string.

What happened …

The apple and the banana balanced because they are both attracted to the center of the earth. The distances they are hung from the center of the measuring stick tell the relative weights of the two objects. The object that is farthest from the center is the lighter of the two objects. We cannot tell you which is heavier, the banana or the apple, because it depends on the sizes of the two pieces of fruit you chose.

Now try this …

You can figure out the weight of one of the objects you chose if you know the weight of the other object. Make a note of where on the measuring stick each object had to hang to make the stick balance.

14

Take one object and weigh it. Then use the following formula to figure out the weight of the other object:

(inch-position of the banana) × (weight of the banana) = (inch-position of the apple) × (weight of the apple)

For example, say the banana was at the 8-inch (20-cm) position and weighed 5 ounces (142 g). If the apple balances at the 10-inch (25-cm) position, then

8 inches (20 cm) × 5 ounces (142 g) = 10 inches (25 cm) × ? ounces (? g)

so

$8 \times 5 = 10x$
$40 = 10x$
$40/10 = x$
$x = 4$ oz

or

$20 \times 142 = 25x$
$2840 = 25x$
$2840/25 = x$
$x = 114$ g

The apple must weigh 4 ounces (114 g).

A DANCING FROG'S LEG

The Electric Battery and Electromagnetism

The Italian scientist Luigi Galvani (1731–1798) is known for his discoveries leading to the first demonstration of an electric current. In 1786 he got a shocking surprise when he saw a leg cut from a dead frog twitching as it lay by itself on a table near an **electrostatic generator**, a machine that produces **electric charges**. Have you ever felt a shock when you walked on a carpet and then touched a wall? If so, you have demonstrated static electricity—the same kind that electrostatic generators produce. **Static electricity** happens when many magnetic particles combine to make one big electric charge.

When he saw the frog's leg twitch, Galvani set out to find the cause. During his experiments, he discovered that the frog's leg also twitched when it was hung from an iron railing by a brass hook and the lower part of the leg came in contact with another part of the iron railing.

Galvani's reports interested another Italian scientist, Alessandro Volta. Volta figured out that the frog's leg on the iron railing twitched because of the difference between the two metals (the brass, which is mainly *copper*, of the hook and the *iron* of the railing). The two metals were accidentally connected through the fluids in the frog's leg. Volta decided that the frog's muscles and nerves represented an

brass hook

frog's leg

iron railing

extremely sensitive **electroscope** (an instrument that detects electric charges). The frog's leg actually detected an electric charge much weaker than any that had been detected before.

Volta went on to prove his theory that different metals have different electric charges by inventing the first practical **battery**. (A battery stores electric charges.) Volta's first step in making his battery was to put moistened cardboard between two different metals, silver and zinc. This combination of two metals with the cardboard in between is called a **cell**. He then connected several of these cells together in a particular order, and this made the complete battery. The power (**voltage**) of the battery depended on the number of galvanic cells connected together. (Notice that these electrical terms were named after Galvani and Volta.) Many of our present-day batteries are still made in a similar way.

Batteries produced in this way were the first source of a useful **electric current** (a constant flow of magnetic particles). Electrostatic generators could not make a continuous current, and they were bulky and hard to move around. Think how easy it is to carry around a flashlight today, with batteries inside it!

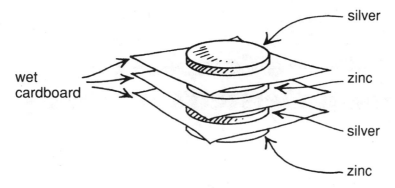

silver

zinc

silver

zinc

wet
cardboard

The parts that combine to form a battery.

Electromagnetism

At the beginning of the nineteenth century, an important connection between electricity and magnetism was discovered by Danish physicist Hans Christian Oersted.

One day, Oersted happened to pass a wire over a compass. The wire carried an electric current, and he noticed that the magnetic needle of the compass moved. From this accident, Oersted realized that an electric current can act like a magnet. Stories tell of Oersted making the discovery while teaching a class, but it is not clear from Oersted's writings whether he actually made the discovery during one of his classes or first demonstrated it there. Whether he made the discovery in the lab or in the class, it was an accidental discovery. It was also a very important discovery, because it led directly to the invention in 1825 of the practical electromagnet by William Sturgeon (an English shoemaker).

An electromagnet is made by surrounding an iron core with a coil of wire that has an electric current running through it. The magnet is much stronger when the electricity is flowing. Electromagnets are used for many things ranging from doorbells and stereo speakers to electric motors of all kinds.

PLEASE BE CAREFUL when doing the experiments in this chapter! Electricity can be dangerous. Don't ever open up a battery. Don't use old batteries, and don't use batteries over 6 volts.

HOW YOU CAN ...

Make a Compass and Repeat Oersted's Discovery

What you need ...

bowl, about 4 to 6 inches (10 to 15 cm) in diameter at the top

tap water

small sewing needle

(if needed) tweezers

(if needed) thin slice of cork (have an adult cut this with a razor blade from a whole cork)

small magnet (like the kind used to hold memos on the refrigerator)

compass

6-volt lantern battery

2 insulated (wrapped in plastic) copper wires, 12 inches (31 cm) long (ask an adult to scrape about ½ inch (1 cm) of the insulation off both ends)

What you do ...

1. Fill the bowl almost to the top with water.

2. Place the needle on a flat surface and rub it with the magnet several times in one direction only.

3. Place the needle *gently* on the surface of the water. [If you drop it from a height of more than ¼ inch (about ½ cm), it will sink to the bottom.] You may have to hold the needle with tweezers to do this. If you still have difficulty, push the needle through the slice of cork so it will float on the water.

4. The needle will align itself in a north/south direction. You can

20

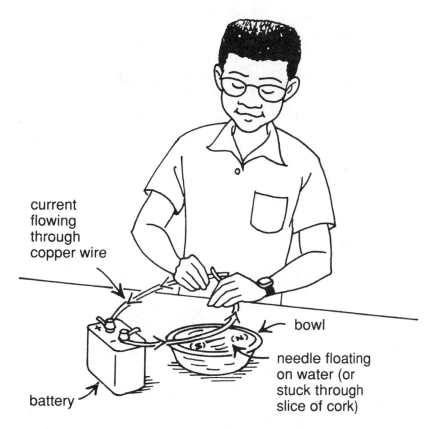

current
flowing
through
copper wire

bowl

needle floating
on water (or
stuck through
slice of cork)

battery

confirm this by comparing its direction with that of an ordinary compass needle.

5. Connect one end of each of the two wires to the two battery terminals and place them and the battery close to the floating needle. Connect the two wires so that they meet about 6 inches (15 cm) above the floating needle (but not in the water). You should see the needle jump, just as Oersted did. Do not leave the two wires connected, since this will ruin the battery after a short time.

What happened ...

A magnetic field is produced by the moving electrons in an electric current. (An **electron** is a tiny magnetic particle.) An electric current flows from one end of the battery to the other. This magnetic field affects the floating needle and makes it jump. You may also test the effect of the battery current on the ordinary compass needle.

HOW YOU CAN ...

Make an Electromagnet

What you need ...

large [3 to 4 inches (8 to 10 cm) long] bolt, about ¼ inch (0.5 cm) thick

an insulated wire at least 4 to 5 feet (120 to 150 cm) long

6-volt lantern battery

What you do ...

1. Wind the insulated wire around the bolt, leaving just enough wire on each end to attach to the 6-volt battery.

2. Attach one end of the wire to one end of the battery and the other end of the wire to the other end of the battery.

What happened ...

When you connected the two ends of the wire to the battery terminals, the bolt acted as a magnet. It is weak, but it will pick up small nails or tacks. The longer the wire you wrap around the bolt and the higher the voltage of the battery, the stronger your magnet will be. Commercial electromagnets like the ones used in motors have many, many feet of thin wire wrapped around a central bar of iron.

PICTURE THIS

Daguerre Invents Photography

Have you ever wondered why you never saw a photograph of George Washington, although you have seen many photographs of Abraham Lincoln? (The familiar picture of Washington on the dollar bill is a portrait painted by Gilbert Stuart.) The explanation is that the first successful photographic process wasn't invented until 1838, after Washington's death, by L. J. M. Daguerre. When you think about it, you will realize that we were at the mercy of artists and their interpretations of the way famous people looked until Daguerre made his accidental discovery!

Daguerre made his first photograph using an improved **camera obscura.** The original camera obscura was a box with a lens in one end and a ground glass plate at the other. The image the camera focused on was displayed upside down on the glass plate. Daguerre's camera obscura had a mirror inside that flipped the image so it was right side up. People used the camera obscura for tracing objects and scenes by placing a sheet of thin paper over the glass plate, but the image could not be **fixed**, or saved on the paper, like a photograph.

One of the first to attempt to fix the image of the camera obscura was another Frenchman, J. N. Niépce. He used a material called asphaltum. In this way he was able to obtain a semipermanent image from the camera obscura in about 1822. This was probably the world's first photograph, but the picture was not very good and the process was hard to do.

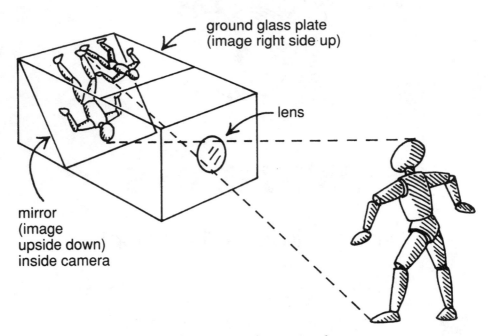

Daguerre's improved camera obscura.

Meanwhile, Daguerre had been experimenting. He tried using silver salts, which could be changed into shiny silver by light, to fix photographic images. But these images were too dim.

Daguerre next took plates of silver-plated copper and exposed them to iodine vapor, which made a thin layer of silver iodide on the surface. Using the camera obscura, he exposed these plates to light and produced a faint image. He tried many ways of intensifying this image, but with little success. One day he placed an exposed plate, one that had only a faint image on it and that he intended to clean and use again, in a cupboard containing various chemicals. After several days, Daguerre removed the plate and found to his amazement that it bore a strong image on its surface!

Daguerre concluded that one or more of the chemicals in the cabinet must have somehow intensified the image. Unfortunately, the cabinet was full of chemicals. With great patience Daguerre began removing the chemicals from the cabinet, one each day, and placing in the cabinet each day an exposed silver iodide plate. But when all of the chemicals had been removed, the image-intensification still occurred! Daguerre examined the cabinet carefully. He found a few drops of mercury on one of the shelves, spilled from a broken thermometer. He concluded that the vapor of the mercury was responsible for the intensified image and he proved it by experiment.

The "daguerreotype," the first true photograph, named after Daguerre, was the result. The standard process for developing a daguerreotype was to place an exposed plate over a cup of mercury heated to about 75° Celsius (167° Fahrenheit). WARNING: DON'T TRY THIS AT HOME, because mercury is very dangerous, especially when heated. Many daguerreotype workers suffered severe illness and some even died because of mercury vapor.

The daguerreotype was an instant success, mainly because the process caught the attention of several famous scientists in Paris. The new photographic process quickly became popular and fashionable in England and America as well as in France. Many improvements in photography came quickly after Daguerre's pioneering work. The most important improvement was the negative/positive process. The daguerreotype was a positive image, meaning that light areas in the things being photographed were light in the daguerreotype. Extra prints could not be made conveniently from positive images. Many positive prints can be made from a negative image (where light areas appear dark). The process by which a negative image was made was invented in England a few years later.

More and more improvements have been made to photography to the point where now everyone can easily take a friend's picture and see it printed minutes later. But it was the public fascination with the first daguerreotype that gave a tremendous boost to early photography. Remember that the discovery that made Daguerre famous was lucky, because he accidentally happened to place his exposed plate in a cabinet containing spilled mercury. But it was Daguerre's intelligence and careful experimentation that led to his success.

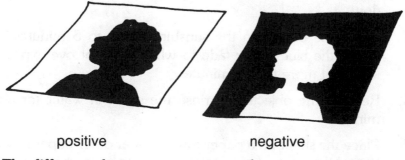

positive   negative

The difference between a positive and a negative image.

HOW YOU CAN ...

Produce a Simple Photographic Image

What you need ...

Sunprint Kit (an inexpensive kit that can be purchased at a toy store)

piece of cardboard

some flat objects, such as keys, coins, paper clips, leaves, lace scraps, or anything with an interesting pattern or shape

paper towels

heavy book

What you do ...

1. Place a blue sheet of paper from the kit on the cardboard, blue side up.

2. Arrange the object(s) on the blue sheet.

3. Put the clear acrylic sheet from the kit over the objects.

4. Place the paper and its components in the sunlight, either outside or on a table or ledge where the sun shines through a window.

5. Leave the objects in the sunshine for 1 to 5 minutes as you watch the blue paper fade to white. Do not overexpose it by leaving it more than 5 minutes.

6. Remove the objects and rinse the sheet in water for about 1 minute.

7. Place the sheet on a paper towel, put another paper towel over it, and then put a heavy book on top to press the paper flat.

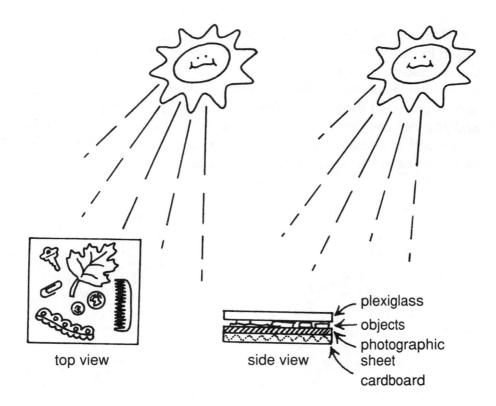

top view   side view

plexiglass
objects
photographic sheet
cardboard

8. After a few minutes, remove the book and the paper towel and allow the sheet to dry completely.

What happened ...

There are special chemicals on the blue paper that react to sunlight and water. Because of these chemicals, the paper turned white in the sunlight except underneath the objects. The objects blocked the light from the sun so it didn't reach the chemicals in those areas under the objects. After being rinsed in water and dried, the part of the paper that turned white turned darker than it was to begin with. The parts of the paper that were underneath the objects ended up being lighter than the surrounding paper.

The process used to make your sunprint is similar to the way photographs are made today. The sunprint has a light background with dark shapes when it is exposed to light (like a negative image), and then changes to a dark background with light shapes when it is rinsed in water (like a positive image). When you take a photograph with a modern-day camera, you expose the film to light. This makes a negative image on the film. When the film is being developed, a light is projected through the film onto special photographic paper, and the negative image is transferred to the paper. The paper is rinsed with chemicals, and the negative image changes to a positive one because of the action of the chemicals.

COW MEDICINE

Jenner and the Discovery of Vaccination

Millions of lives have been saved through the use of penicillin (which was discovered accidentally) and other germ-killing drugs, but even more people have been saved from disease by **vaccination**. Vaccination, also discovered accidentally, is a special procedure that prevents people from getting certain diseases. Germ-killing drugs cure diseases that people already have.

Edward Jenner discovered vaccination by accident. Jenner was born in 1749 in Gloustershire, England, a region with many dairy farms. When he was only 19 and studying medicine with a local doctor, he happened to talk with a woman who used to be a milkmaid. She told him that she could never get smallpox because she had had cowpox, which she had gotten from milking cows. Smallpox was one of the most deadly diseases to humans.

Jenner thought this was interesting, but he was too busy with his studies to think any more about it at the time. But a few years later, when Jenner was working as a doctor, he realized how impossible it was to treat patients with smallpox. They would die from the disease no matter what he did. He remembered what the milkmaid had said about cowpox and smallpox and decided to investigate.

He checked with the milkmaids in his area and discovered that they hardly ever got smallpox. This gave Jenner the idea that he

could introduce the cowpox germs into people's bodies and that this might prevent them from getting smallpox. The dose of cowpox would be mild and would not hurt the person exposed to it. The person's body would manufacture **antibodies** to fight the disease. Jenner reasoned that these antibodies would also fight off smallpox.

In 1796, he tried out his theory. He scratched some matter from a milkmaid's cowpox blisters into the skin of an eight-year-old boy. Two months later, the boy was carefully exposed to smallpox, but he did not develop the disease. Jenner took a big chance in exposing the boy to smallpox, but at the time it seemed the only way to prove his theory. If it were successful, it would save many lives.

After a second successful test of his theory, Jenner wrote a pamphlet to announce his discovery. Another doctor in London was also able to carry out several successful tests of Jenner's method. This doctor told other doctors and the word eventually spread all over the world. Jenner received many honors because of his discovery, and other doctors began to search for similar ways to prevent other diseases. Today, we have vaccinations for mumps, measles, tuberculosis, and even influenza (the flu).

Jenner himself never used the word *vaccination* for his procedure. Instead he used **inoculation** or sometimes *variolae vaccinae*, the Latin term for cowpox. Louis Pasteur, a French scientist, suggested the term *vaccination* for all such procedures in honor of Jenner. The word **vaccine** is now used to describe the specially prepared germs that are used in any inoculation.

HOW YOU CAN ...

Help Prevent the Common Cold

The vaccination that Jenner discovered was one way to prevent a very serious disease. There are other simple ways to prevent more common illnesses for which there is no cure, such as the common cold.

One way to avoid catching a cold is to wash your hands often to get rid of any germs. Doctors believe that we catch more colds by touching than in any other way.

If you do get sick, you can make sure you don't spread your germs to others by staying home from school when you have a cold. (This shouldn't be too hard to do!)

THE CASE OF THE MELTING MAILBAGS

Goodyear and the Vulcanization of Rubber

In the early sixteenth century, Spanish explorers found South American Indians playing games with a ball formed by hardening the vegetable gum (called *latex*) that oozed from certain trees. Although the Spanish explorers brought some of this "India gum" back to Europe, they couldn't think of a good use for it. Then Joseph Priestley, the man who discovered oxygen, showed that it could be used to rub out lead pencil marks. Ever since then, this material has been called *rubber*.

The main reason that Europeans couldn't find an important use for rubber for more than two centuries was that rubber became soft and sticky at high temperatures and stiff and brittle at low temperatures. The Scottish scientist Charles Macintosh discovered one of the few good uses for India rubber. He coated two pieces of cloth with rubber and pressed them together with the rubber in the middle to act as glue. This made the double fabric waterproof and it was used to make raincoats. This is how the macintosh was invented. The name is still used in England for rainwear made of all sorts of modern fabrics.

Boots and shoes made of rubber or rubber-coated fabric were first made in the United States in the 1830s. Americans, however, soon became disgusted with shoes that became stiff in winter and soft and shapeless in summer.

At this point, Charles Goodyear entered the scene. Goodyear was born in 1800 in New Haven, Connecticut, the son of an unsuccessful merchant and inventor. The younger Goodyear became fascinated with the possibility of somehow making rubber less sensitive to temperature changes, so that it would be useful in many ways. This fascination became a compulsion, one that used up the little wealth that Goodyear had. Between 1830 and 1839, Goodyear was put in prison more than once for owing people money. He became dependent on relatives for food and shelter, but still his obsession with rubber continued.

One of his disasters during this time was to sell the government a large order of mailbags that had been coated with rubber to make them waterproof. To Goodyear's horror, the mailbags turned sticky and shapeless from heat before they even left the factory.

After many more unsuccessful attempts to treat rubber, one of which involved mixing it with sulfur, Goodyear accidentally allowed a mixture of rubber and sulfur to come in contact with the surface of a hot stove. To his surprise, the rubber did not melt, but only charred slightly, as a piece of leather would.

Goodyear immediately understood the significance of this accident. That night he nailed the piece of gum outside in the intense cold. When he brought it inside in the morning, it was still just as flexible as it had been when he put it out.

We now know the chemical reason why heating rubber with sulfur makes the rubber more useful. The sulfur **atoms** form links between the long chains of rubber **molecules**. These links make the material less sensitive to changes in temperature.

By further tests, Goodyear determined the best temperature and time for heating rubber with sulfur, and the amounts of rubber and sulfur to use. He applied for a patent that was granted in 1844 for a process that he called **vulcanization** after the Roman god of fire, Vulcan.

It would be pleasant to think that Goodyear "lived happily ever after" after his discovery of the vulcanization process, but this was not the case. He had to defend his patent many times against people who wanted to steal his process, and he never did recover from his huge debts. However, the vulcanization process did lead to great activity in the manufacture and use of rubber, especially in tires. The Goodyear Tire and Rubber Company was named after Charles Goodyear.

HOW YOU CAN ...

Test Rubber

Today almost all rubber goods are made of vulcanized rubber, so it is not easy to show how important Goodyear's discovery of the vulcanization process was. However, even vulcanized rubber is more *elastic* when warm than when cold. You can demonstrate this quite easily by showing how high warm and cold rubber balls will bounce.

What you need ...

2 new tennis balls (or any rubber balls that will bounce to the same height when dropped from the same height)

What you do ...

1. Hold the two balls over your head at the same height and drop them on a hard-surfaced floor, such as a bare wooden or cement floor. Be sure that they bounce to the same height.

2. Put one of the balls in your freezer and leave it there for 1 hour.

3. Keep the second ball at room temperature.

4. Remove the cold ball and immediately drop it and the other ball from the same height over your head.

What happened ...

The cold ball did not bounce nearly as high as the warmer ball. This is because even after vulcanization, rubber is not as elastic when cold as when warm. If a material is more elastic, this means that it can more easily return to its former shape after being stretched or flattened. When a rubber ball bounces, it is flattened slightly when it hits the floor, and how high it bounces depends on how fast it returns to its round shape when it bounces up. Therefore, a warmer, more elastic ball will bounce higher than a colder, less elastic ball. Without vulcanization, the cold ball would not have bounced at all.

A SMASHING DISCOVERY

Benedictus Invents Safety Glass

Natural glass (such as obsidian) has been present since the formation of our planet. Obsidian and other types of natural glass were formed from common **elements** in the earth's crust by intense volcanic heat followed by rapid cooling.

The origin of the first **synthetic** (man-made) glass is unknown. One of the most common legends about the accidental creation of man-made glass was documented by Pliny the Elder, a Roman scholar and historian who lived in the first century A.D. He died during the volcanic eruption of Mount Vesuvius in 79 A.D.

Pliny credited Phoenician merchants with producing glass accidentally. (Phoenicia was an ancient country located where Syria and Lebanon now have their seacoasts.) These merchants made a fire on a sandy beach and rested their cooking pots on blocks of natron (a mineral made of sodium carbonate). They let the fire burn overnight, and in the morning, to their amazement, they found molten glass glistening among the ashes. The heat had fused the natron blocks with the silica of the sand. Although this accidental discovery and its date cannot be proved (it has been estimated at about 4000 B.C.), we do know that Egyptians used glass bottles as early as 1500 B.C.

The accidental discovery of safety glass occurred at the time it was most needed—soon after the invention of automobiles, which had glass windshields. Automobiles were much more likely than horse-drawn buggies to go out of control and crash, and broken windshields could cause serious injury to people in the cars.

In 1903 a French chemist named Edouard Benedictus dropped a glass flask on a hard floor. The flask shattered, but Benedictus noticed to his surprise that the broken pieces of glass did not fly apart. Instead the flask remained almost in its original shape. Benedictus examined the flask and found that there was a thin plastic film on the inside to which the broken pieces of glass were stuck. He realized that this film had been left behind by the evaporation of a liquid containing some **collodion** (a thick gluelike plastic made from cotton and nitric acid), which the flask had contained. Benedictus made a note of the incident on a label attached to the flask, but thought no more about it at that time.

Soon after this laboratory accident, however, Benedictus read an account of a young girl who had been badly cut by glass in an automobile accident in Paris. A few weeks later, he read of another such accident. He realized that his experience with the nonshattering glass flask offered a potential solution to such problems. He rushed to

cracked glass
held together
by collodion

glass ← → / cellulose nitrate

The first safety glass was a "sandwich" of two pieces of glass with a sheet of cellulose nitrate between them.

his laboratory, found the labeled flask, and spent the night planning how a coating of some kind could be applied to make glass safe. It is said that by evening of the same day he had produced the first sheet of safety glass.

The new safety glass was given the name "triplex" because it was made of three sheets of material. The triplex glass was a sandwich in which two sheets of glass acted as the bread, and the meat was a sheet of cellulose nitrate placed between them. The three sheets of transparent material were bonded together by heat.

Although Benedictus invented safety glass to prevent injury from flying glass from automobile windshields, it was not widely used for this purpose until the 1920s. At that time, the number of automobiles and their speed increased greatly, and injury caused by glass became a serious problem. Then laminated (triplex-type) windshields became standard in American automobiles.

Other Improvements

Another form of safety glass is called *tempered glass*. This glass doesn't contain a plastic inner film. Instead, it has been treated by heat in such a way that when it breaks, it shatters into many small pieces. These small pieces are less likely to be harmful than are large pieces of glass. Tempered glass is used in the side and back windows of automobiles, but in the United States and in some other countries, laminated glass is required for windshields.

Aircraft require very strong windows that must resist extremes of temperature and pressure as well as high-speed bird impact! These requirements are met by highly specialized windshields that consist of several layers of glass and plastic of various thicknesses.

HOW YOU CAN ...

Perform an Experiment Like Benedictus' Discovery of Safety Glass

What you need ...

night-light (the type that uses a 7-watt, 120- or 130-volt bulb)

clear fingernail polish that contains cellulose nitrate (although it may be labeled [incorrectly] "nitrocellulose." This is exactly what Benedictus had in his flask.)

safety goggles

What you do ...

1. Screw the bulb into the night-light. THE NIGHT-LIGHT SHOULD NOT BE PLUGGED IN.

2. Paint the bulb heavily with the clear fingernail polish.

3. Allow the polish to dry enough so that it will not drip.

4. Plug the night-light into an electric outlet and leave it turned on long enough to finish the drying of the polish as it gets warm.

5. When the polish is dry, unplug the night-light from the electrical outlet.

6. Let the bulb cool, then unscrew it from the socket.

7. Put on the safety goggles and drop the bulb onto a hard surface.

What happened ...

If the fingernail polish was thick enough, the glass of the bulb shattered, but the bulb did not lose its shape. The plastic of the fingernail polish held the bulb together. This is the way safety glass works. If the bulb broke, try the experiment again, coating the new bulb more thickly with the fingernail polish. Be sure to sweep up any broken glass.

DIGS, FINDS, CAVES, AND DIVES

How to Succeed in Archaeology Without Really Trying

Mary Leakey, an **archaeologist** (a person who studies things like bones, buildings, and tools for clues about past human life) once said: "In **archaeology** you almost never find what you set out to find." She could have also said the opposite of this, that many famous archaeological discoveries have been made by people who had no intention of finding anything of historical interest—that is, by serendipity!

Accidental discoveries in archaeology have provided us with information about ancient civilizations, prehistoric cultures, early technology, and religious history, among many other things. Let's look at some of the ways in which these lucky discoveries were made.

Digs That Produced Unexpected Results

Herculaneum and Pompeii

In 79 A.D. the volcano Vesuvius erupted, burying the neighboring cities of Herculaneum and Pompeii. The rain of lava and ashes was so quick and devastating that the buildings and people of these neigh-

45

boring cities were instantaneously buried and frozen in time for 17 centuries. Over the centuries, dirt was washed down from the surrounding mountains and the area became farmland. Then, in 1709, a peasant who was digging a well in the farmland above Herculaneum brought up fragments of marble sculpture. An Italian prince learned of this, bought the land, and brought workers to dig at the location. They found several complete female sculptures. It turned out that the prince's workers had dug into the theater of Herculaneum.

The news of the buried cities spread. The Italian King Charles III hired a Spanish engineer to dig up and move every treasure that was portable to his private museum. A century later, the French came upon the ruins of Herculaneum. The careless **excavations** of the French government were as bad as those of the Italians before them. Statues and paintings on walls were removed from the temples and the exposed buildings were left to decay.

Finally, in 1860 King Victor Emmanuel II ascended the throne of Italy. He encouraged careful excavations at Pompeii under the direction of Giuseppe Fiorelli, a professor who knew the history of Pompeii. Fiorelli developed a clever procedure for producing plaster forms of the bodies that had been encased in lava but had decayed during the centuries, leaving hollow shells. The shells were filled with plaster. After the plaster had hardened, the lava and ash molds were carefully chipped away, leaving lifelike forms of the people in the positions they were in when the volcano's ash buried them.

Three-fourths of Pompeii's area has been uncovered and cleared now, including two theaters and the civic forum. The rest of the city still lies buried beneath the houses and gardens of the present Italian town. The nearby brooding volcano still smokes from time to time, although there hasn't been a major eruption since 1944.

Mammoths in the Black Hills

In 1974, while digging foundations for a new housing development near the Black Hills of South Dakota, George Hanson uncovered a strange group of bones about 20 feet (6.1 m) beneath the surface. Hanson's son reported the find to his former professor, Larry Agenbroad, who recognized the bones as those of Columbian **mammoths** (huge extinct animals similar to elephants). The mammoths had been trapped in a water-filled hole some 26,000 years ago. Their preserved bones, or fossils, lay in the positions in which the huge prehistoric animals died. A museum now stands at the site where you can see the fossils, and digging still continues at the site one month each year.

Mastodons in Austin

A similar event occurred in the authors' home city of Austin, Texas, in January of 1985. While excavating for the foundation of an office building, a backhoe operator unearthed a well-preserved ivory tusk. An archaeologist on the site during the excavation identified the tusk as belonging to a **mastodon**. Mastodons were prehistoric animals, like the mammoths, related to present day elephants.

Mastodon fossils are even rarer than those of mammoths. Only a few hundred mastodons have been found, whereas over three thou-

An American mastodon.

sand mammoths have been unearthed. Tusks of three mastodons were found at the Austin site, as well as a rib, part of an upper left jawbone with two large teeth intact, spinal bones, a leg bone, and a foot bone. One of the two teeth was a molar that was so well preserved that it was shiny after washing.

The site was thought to be the bed of a pond along the old flood plain of the Colorado River, which flows through Austin. The bones probably settled there after being washed downstream from where the mastodon actually died. Scientists estimated their age at about fifteen thousand years.

Interesting Characters That Turned Up

Some of the most important archaeological discoveries that gave us evidence of the earliest humans were also made by accident.

The Taung Child

In 1924, workers were excavating for lime in the Taung cave near Johannesburg, South Africa. Suddenly, one of the miners saw something resembling a small (human?) brain among the limestone rocks. He took it to the mine office, where a message was sent to Professor Raymond Dart, an expert in **anatomy** (the study of the body parts of humans and animals). Soon Dart announced the discovery of an almost complete skull of a child. The skull came from the limestone found in the Taung cave. This child represented the oldest human ancestor known at that time—more than a million years old. (A spectacular picture of the Taung child's skull was reproduced on the cover of the November 1985 issue of *National Geographic* magazine.)

Dart, as it turned out, was exactly the right person to turn an accidental find into a major scientific discovery. He had the intelligence and curiosity to recognize this ancient child as what some have called "the missing link" between our nonhuman and human ancestors. Dart's ideas stirred up a lot of controversy, but later discoveries in Africa proved most of Dart's claims to be correct.

Lucy

Nature has sometimes helped reveal past history to archaeologists. An excellent example is the story of Lucy (a prehistoric human). Lucy was found by archaeologists seeking someone like her, but she wouldn't have been found without some extra help from Mother Nature.

In November 1974, archaeologist Donald Johanson and a graduate student, Tom Gray, were searching for ancient human fossils in north-central Ethiopia. All they were finding were the bones of animals. Then one day while walking along a gully they noticed a bone sticking out from the eroded slope above them. Although it had been buried under layers of sediment and volcanic ash for millions of years, a recent flash flood had washed the dirt off of this bone just in time for the archaeologists to find it. And they found not just one bone, but many more. After three weeks of excavation, Johanson and his colleagues found several hundred pieces of bones. When the bones were pieced together, they formed a single human skeleton—an adult female only 3 feet 8 inches (112 cm) tall. This individual was named Lucy.

Lucy stirred up great excitement because she represented the most complete and oldest prehistoric human ancestor known at that time. Scientists estimate her age at about three million years.

An Unusual Object That Came to Light: The Rosetta Stone

Perhaps the ultimate accidental archaeological discovery is the Rosetta Stone. This stone was the key that unlocked the history of ancient Egypt, one of the world's greatest early civilizations. The discovery occurred when a French soldier came across the stone while making repairs to a fort near the town of Rosetta, in Egypt. The officer in charge of the repairs realized the importance of the stone, which was part of an old wall they were about to destroy. He saved the stone from being demolished with the rest of the wall.

French soldiers discover the Rosetta Stone.

The officer realized that the stone contained the same information in three different languages. One of the languages was **hieroglyphics** (ancient Egyptian writing) which no one then was able to read. Another of the languages was Greek. Since Greek was a well-known language, it could be used to translate the hieroglyphics. This allowed people to understand, for the first time, the hieroglyphics found all over Egypt.

Boys and Caves

The curiosity of boys about caves led to the discovery of valuable archaeological information on at least two occasions.

Lascaux Cave

In 1940, four teenage boys were exploring the woods near the town of Montignac in southwestern France when they discovered a small hole in the ground. They enlarged the hole enough to allow them to crawl inside and found a narrow passage that led into a large underground cave. With the light of their oil lantern, they were amazed to see brilliantly colored paintings of animals on the white limestone walls and ceiling of the cave. They reported their discovery to their former schoolmaster, who made a telephone call to the Abbe Henri Breuil, an expert on prehistoric art.

Breuil came to see the cave paintings and proclaimed them to be truly ancient. Modern methods of archaeological dating proved the paintings to have been made about 17,000 years ago. When news of the discovery reached the public, archaeologists, journalists, and sightseers came to the cave. Since that time, thousands of tourists have come to marvel at the prehistoric artwork. They now can view an exact replica that has been built next to the original cave. The replica was built so that there would be no danger of damaging the irreplaceable original artwork.

The head of the present-day guides, who show the authentic cave with special care and knowledge only to those authorized to see it, is Jacques Marsal. At the age of 15, Jacques was one of the boys who found the cave.

The Dead Sea Scrolls

In 1947, a Bedouin boy was searching for a goat that had strayed among the barren cliffs bordering the northwest coast of the Dead Sea. He noticed a small opening in one of the cliffs and tossed a stone into it, only to hear the shattering of pottery inside. He was startled by the sound but, as it was late in the evening, he waited for another day to explore. The next day was devoted to watering his flocks, but two days later he returned to the site, hoping he might find gold in the cave. With difficulty, he managed to crawl inside the cave, where he found several large earthen jars. In one of these he found two aged scrolls of parchment wrapped in linen and a roll of leather.

The Bedouin boy called his two older companions and they took the scrolls and the leather roll back to their camp. Eventually, they were sold to the Syrian archbishop in Jerusalem, who realized they were historically important.

Although a series of experts who examined the scroll manuscripts pronounced them to be worthless, the archbishop persisted. He sent them to the American School of Oriental Research in Jerusalem. It was there that the archaic (very old) forms of the Hebrew letters on the scrolls convinced visiting American scholars Drs. John C. Trever and William Brownlee of the sensational nature of the documents. They made photographs of sections of one scroll (a copy of the Biblical book of Isaiah) and sent them to Dr. William F. Albright, an authority on old Hebrew language. Dr. Albright promptly dated the manuscript at about 100 B.C. and called the scrolls "an absolutely incredible find." These scrolls were a thousand years older than all but a few fragmentary Biblical manuscripts previously known. The newly found scrolls filled in important gaps in our knowledge of the Bible.

Fighting between Arabs and Jews delayed further investigation by archaeologists until 1949. The initial searches for more scrolls and for information about the people who had prepared and hid them failed. However, the poor people of the region saw the possibility of a new source of income. (The Bedouin had sold the original scrolls to the eager Jerusalem scholars.) They busily began to search the thousands of cracks and fissures in the barren desert wilderness cliffs near the Dead Sea. In 1952, they struck pay dirt less than a mile from the original finding by the Bedouin boy.

Further intense activity by both Bedouin and archaeologists dis-

A Bedouin boy discovers the Dead Sea Scrolls.

closed the remains of an ancient settlement of Jewish monks known as Essenes. It was the Essenes who produced the scrolls and hid them, apparently intending to return for them after the Roman persecution. For some reason, they never did. Several other caves that contained ancient manuscripts were also found, including one that contained the monks' main library.

In all, thousands of fragments of nearly 400 separate scrolls have been found, including portions of every book of the Old Testament except Esther. Decades may pass before we can understand the full significance of the scrolls.

Sponge Divers

Another source of information about ancient civilizations lies at the bottom of the seas. We have learned much by finding ships that sank centuries ago and have preserved records of the times in which they sailed. Until very recently, with the development of sophisticated instruments such as magnetometers, sonar, and remote-control video cameras, the most common source of oceanic discovery was the sponge diver of the Mediterranean Sea. Many times these divers have found wrecked ships, or signs of them, while bringing up sponges from the sea floor at depths of over 100 feet (30.5 m).

A Bronze-Age Ship Off the Turkish Coast

Peter Throckmorton, an American diver, was exploring off the Turkish coast in the summer of 1958 without much success. However, an idle mention by one of the local sponge divers of corroded copper ingots shaped like animal hides brought the American and his crew back the next summer. When they looked where the sponge diver said he had seen the ingots, they found the wreckage site of a ship from the Bronze Age (the ancient time in human history when bronze tools were used).

Although they could not find the actual ship that year, they recovered many copper ingots, bronze spear points and axes, and crude pottery items. The ship itself (or at least fragments of its hull) was located in 1969. Divers also found enough examples of the ship's cargo to date the last voyage of the ship at about 1200 B.C. More than a ton of bronze and copper objects from the ship's cargo was placed in a museum in Bodrum, Turkey.

A Greek Ship Off Cyprus

A Greek ship that sank off the coast of Cyprus in the fourth century B.C. was discovered in 1967. Here, too, the key to the discovery was the sighting by a sponge diver of a mass of **amphorae** (pottery jars used for wine at that time). These jars were often carried as cargo on merchant ships of the Mediterranean. The wooden hull of the ship was virtually intact. It had been preserved by the sand that had covered it for 22 centuries, as well as by a shell of lead that had been intended to protect the wood from shipworms. Apparently, the ship's crew had put too much faith in the lead shield. The archaeologists found that the worms had done extensive damage beneath the lead. The tunneling by the worms underneath the lead, where it would not be noticed, might have caused the sinking of the ship.

HOW YOU CAN ...

Make Plaster Forms from a Mold

What you need ...

plastic candy mold with several shapes (can be found at craft stores)

petroleum jelly (such as Vaseline®)

plaster of Paris

2-cup measuring cup

1-cup measuring cup

tap water

teaspoon

What you do ...

1. Coat the insides of the shapes in the candy mold with petroleum jelly. Also coat the edges around the shapes.

2. Measure 1 cup of plaster of Paris in the small measuring cup and pour it into the large measuring cup.

3. Measure ½ cup of tap water in the small measuring cup and pour this into the large measuring cup.

4. Stir the mixture well with the teaspoon.

5. Pour the plaster mixture into the shapes in the mold, being careful not to let the plaster overflow the mold.

6. Allow the plaster to harden for 24 hours.

7. Turn the mold over and tap on the shapes to loosen the plaster forms from the mold.

What happened ...

The plaster took the same forms as the shapes in the candy mold. In the same way, the plaster Fiorelli used took the forms of human figures when he filled up the lava and ash molds at Pompeii.

BANGS, TWINKLES, AND BUMPS

Astronomical Discoveries

The "Big Bang"

In 1964, Arno Penzias and Robert Wilson, scientists at Bell Laboratories in New Jersey, were modifying a radio antenna that had been used to receive signals from the early communication satellites. (These were rockets that had been sent into space to receive and transmit radio signals between various places on the earth.) They intended to use the antenna for studies on radio signals from outer space. In preparation, they tried to eliminate all **terrestrial** (earthly) sources of background radio signals. They also evicted a pair of pigeons that were nesting in the horn-shaped antenna and removed what they called "a white **dielectric** substance" (pigeon poop). After taking all such precautions, they found that there was still a left-over radiation "noise," comparable to static on a radio, which they thought must come from **radiation** in space.

Astronomers at that time already had a theory that the universe started about 15 billion years ago with a huge explosion. This is called the Big Bang theory. This explosion produced a tremendous radiation of energy, which has been decreasing ever since. James Peebles at Princeton University presented a paper about this theory at a scientific meeting in early 1965. Penzias and Wilson heard of

Peebles' theory about the Big Bang. When the two groups exchanged information, they concluded that the "noise" detected by the Bell radio antenna had just the right amount of energy expected for the radiation left over from the Big Bang. As one scientist said, "Either we've seen the birth of the universe, or we've seen a pile of pigeon———!"

Apparently, the Nobel Prize authorities accepted the more scientific explanation, for Penzias and Wilson were awarded the prize in physics in 1978.

Pulsars

Jocelyn Bell and Anthony Hewish were not trying to discover **pulsars** (remains of exploded stars) in 1967. How could they? No one suspected that they existed. At Cambridge University that summer, Bell and Hewish were trying to measure the size of radio sources by looking at their radio waves. Bell noticed something unusual in the results. Bursts of radiation, or pulses, appeared on the records each midnight. She and Hewish eliminated the possibility that these pulses were coming from earth. They also noted that the pulses began to come earlier each night, just as stars do when they appear.

When the pulses became very strong, the astronomers noticed that they were also very short and came in a regular pattern. Bell searched through hundreds of old charts and found three more pulses. When these findings were announced, many explanations were given. Some even joked that the pulses were "communications from 'Little Green Men' in outer space."

A better answer came from David Staelin and Edward Reifenstein at the National Radio Astronomy Observatory who found a pulsar in the center of the Crab Nebula (a **nebula** is a group of stars). Pulsars were identified as the remains of exploded stars. Because the exploded stars are light years away, the pulses reach us thousands of years after they were sent out by the stars.

Pluto's Moon

In this story of discovery, an accidental mechanical breakdown led someone to realize that a photograph, thought to be accidentally damaged, really was not! In 1978, James Christy at the U.S. Naval Observatory was measuring the orbit of the planet Pluto. To do so, he had placed a photographic plate containing a picture of Pluto on an instrument called a Star Scan machine. When he did this, he noticed a bulge on the edge of the planet. At first he assumed the bulge was an accident, and he was going to throw the photograph away. Luckily, however (as it turned out), the machine began to malfunction

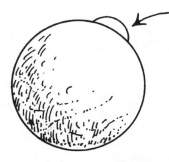

moon behind Pluto

Pluto and its moon.

59

at that instant, and Christy called in an electronics technician to repair it. The technician asked Christy to stand by while he made the repairs, because he thought he might need Christy's help.

While he was waiting, Christy studied the photograph more carefully, and he decided to look through the archives for earlier pictures of the planet. The first one he found was marked "Pluto image. Elongated. Plate no good. Reject." His interest now really aroused, Christy searched through the archives and found six more pictures dated between 1965 and 1970 that showed the same bulge. His further studies proved that the bulge was really a moon of the planet. If the Star Scan machine had not broken down when it did, he would not have discovered the new moon.

HOW YOU CAN …

Explore the Earth's Moon

Most astronomers begin their careers by looking at the earth's moon. After all, it's the nearest space object to earth and many fascinating details can be seen, even with a pair of binoculars. There are still a lot of mysteries in space waiting to be discovered. Maybe you'll be lucky enough to find one!

What you need …

calendar that gives the phases of the moon

binoculars

What you do ...

1. Using your calendar, pick a night just a few nights after the new moon.

2. Go outside on this night (be sure the sky is clear) and look at the moon through the binoculars.

3. Compare what you can see with your naked eye to what you can see with the binoculars. Do you see something different through the binoculars?

What happened ...

On the night you chose after the new moon, you saw a waxing moon. (**Waxing** means getting larger; **waning** means getting smaller.) Through the binoculars, you probably saw the outline of the whole moon, but with your naked eye you only saw the bright part. (The bright part is reflecting the light from the sun.) The magnifying lenses in binoculars make the moon look larger. Binoculars and telescopes make it possible to see details on the moon and other astronomical objects that we can't see with the naked eye. Astronomers can only see and take pictures of things like Pluto's moon with the help of the powerful magnifying lenses in telescopes.

Now try this ...

Go to a bookstore or library and get a book on observing the moon, planets, and stars. Using your binoculars, or a telescope if you have one, start trying to locate the objects described in the book. If you see something that you can't find in a book, tell someone. You may have just discovered something new!

FROM THE MOLDY PAST

Fleming Discovers Penicillin

Perhaps the best-known example of serendipity is Sir Alexander Fleming's accidental discovery of penicillin. Fleming's life is full of apparently unrelated events, without any one of which it would not have reached the climax it did. Some people feel that it couldn't have been just chance that led to Fleming's amazing discovery. It's true that in addition to being lucky, Fleming was also well prepared to see the significance of the accident he observed.

Fleming was born in Scotland in 1881. When he was 16, he took a job in London. He took time, also, to join the London Scottish Volunteers, a group with which he played water polo. At one time, his team played against a team from St. Mary's Hospital. A water polo match may not seem to have anything to do with science, but this game played an important part in the future course of Fleming's life.

A few years after this game, he received a small legacy and was encouraged by his brother to enter a medical school. There were 12 of these in London, and Fleming knew nothing about any of them— except the one connected with St. Mary's Hospital, which he knew had a water polo team. That's why Fleming chose St. Mary's. At the same time, Almroth Wright joined the school as a teacher in **bacteriology**. Fleming first planned to become a surgeon, but he was of-

fered a position in Almroth Wright's laboratory following his gradua-
tion. He worked in that laboratory for the rest of his life.

During World War I, Fleming and Wright were sent to France
where they worked with wounded soldiers. Doctors at that time were
depending on **antiseptics** to cure the battle wounds. But Fleming
observed that **phenol** (carbolic acid), the most common antiseptic at
that time, did more harm than good. It killed the white blood cells
faster than it killed the bacteria. Fleming knew this was bad, because
these cells are the body's natural defenders against bacteria.

Soon after this, Fleming accidentally discovered an **antibiotic**
that killed bacteria but did not harm white blood cells. While he was
examining some bacteria in a dish, a tear fell from his eye into the
dish. The next day when he examined the contents of the dish, he
found a clear space where the tear had fallen. His keen observation
and curiosity led him to the correct conclusion: the tear contained a
substance that caused rapid destruction of the bacteria, but was
harmless to human tissue. He named the antibiotic **enzyme** in the

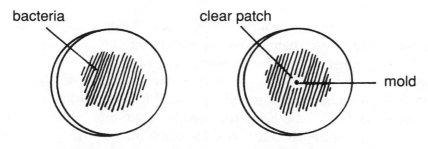

**Fleming noticed a clear patch in one of the bacteria
samples he was studying.**

tear **lysozyme**. This discovery turned out to be of little practical importance, however, because the germs that this antibiotic killed were
relatively harmless, but it was essential to the discovery of penicillin.

In the summer of 1928, Fleming was doing research on influenza (the flu). He was examining some cultures of bacteria grown in
petri dishes (flat glass dishes), with a microscope. Fleming noticed an
unusual clear area in one dish. He found that the clear area sur-
rounded a spot where a bit of mold had fallen into the dish, apparently while the dish had been left uncovered. Fleming concluded that
the mold was producing something that was deadly to the **staphylococcus** bacteria in the culture dish. He reported that if it hadn't been
for his previous experience with lysozyme, he would have thrown the
dish away!

Fleming went on to identify the mold as belonging to the **genus**
Penicillium. He named the antibiotic substance it produced **penicillin**. Later he would say, "There are thousands of different moulds
and there are thousands of different bacteria, and that chance put the
mould in the right spot at the right time was like winning the Irish
sweep" (sweepstakes). Although penicillin is deadly to many bacteria,
including *staphylococcus*, it has no effect on some other types of
(healthy) bacteria. The bacteria that penicillin kills are responsible for
many common and serious human infections.

Lucky Science Strikes Again

It was not easy to produce penicillin in amounts large enough to be
useful in treating disease. Many medical scientists took up the problem of making the use of penicillin practical. Two of these were

Howard W. Florey, a professor at Oxford University, and his co-worker, Ernst Boris Chain, a Jewish refugee from Hitler's Germany.

Florey came to the United States to describe the way penicillin was made in England and to see if there were any new ways to produce it in the United States. Florey asked for help from a man in Washington, D.C., who just happened to know that a U.S. Department of Agriculture laboratory had for some time been trying to find a new use for a thick liquid left over from the corn-milling process. When this liquid was used in the production of penicillin, it made ten times more than they could make before.

And then "Moldy Mary" entered the scene. "Moldy Mary" was actually Mary Hunt. She was given her nickname because of her enthusiasm in searching for new mold sources. Mary found a cantaloupe with a mold growing on it that turned out to produce penicillin twice as successfully as the mold that was being used.

Fleming, Florey, and Chain shared the Nobel Prize in Physiology or Medicine in 1945, and all three were later knighted for their discoveries which resulted in the relief of much suffering and the saving of uncounted lives.

HOW YOU CAN ...

Grow Your Own Mold

What you need ...

grapefruit

magnifying lens

What you do ...

1. Put the grapefruit in an open dish and put it in your bathroom for several days. (Putting it in the bathroom ensures that there is plenty of moisture in the air.)

2. Check the fruit every day for a week.

3. When mold appears on the fruit, examine it through your magnifying lens.

What happened ...

After a few days, the surface of the fruit became moldy. Many different kinds of molds are found in moist air. The kind that grows on grapefruit stayed on the grapefruit and grew. (Be sure that you don't eat the moldy fruit. Throw it away.) You can't make your own penicillin—that takes special equipment.

HOW SWEET IT IS
(AND NONFATTENING)

Three Kinds of Substitute Sugar

The three most common substitutes for sugar—saccharin (Sweet'n Low™), cyclamates, and aspartame (NutraSweet™)—were all discovered by accident.

Saccharin

Saccharin, the first artificial sweetener, was discovered over a hundred years ago, long before it became fashionable to use a substitute for common table sugar (**sucrose**). This happened in the laboratory of Ira Remsen, the most famous American chemist of the nineteenth century.

In 1879, one of Remsen's students, named Fahlberg, noticed that a substance that he had accidentally spilled onto his hand tasted unusually sweet. (Chemists in those days were not nearly so cautious about smelling and tasting the materials they worked with as they are now. Many incautious chemists became ill and some even died as a result. Be sure you don't follow Fahlberg's example! Never taste any unknown substance unless your parent or teacher says it's OK.)

Fahlberg immediately realized the possible importance of the new sweet-tasting substance. He developed a process for making the sub-

stance and took out a patent on it in 1885. The name he chose for it was *saccharin*, from the Latin word for sugar, *saccharum*. Saccharin became popular around 1900 and it is still the most widely used sugar substitute today. It is sold under the brand name Sweet'n Low.

Cyclamates

In 1937, a chemistry student working at the University of Illinois was preparing a series of compounds called sulfamates that were expected to have interesting medical properties. The student, Michael Sveda, noticed a surprisingly sweet taste to a cigarette he was smoking while in the laboratory (another incautious practice!). He traced the source to one of the substances he was preparing. Both the sodium and calcium salts of this substance (called **cyclamates**) were used as sugar substitutes until 1970. At that time they were banned for use in the United States by the Food and Drug Administration because they were found to harm animals.

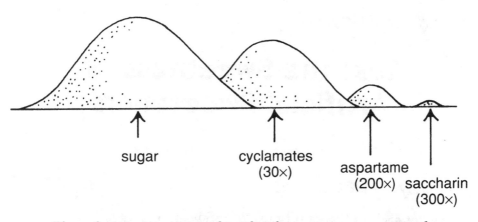

How Sweet It Is (and Nonfattening)

sugar

cyclamates
(30×)

aspartame
(200×) saccharin
(300×)

**The relative sweetness of artificial sweeteners compared
to sucrose (common table sugar): The mound of sugar is
equal in sweetness to the smaller mounds of artificial
sweetners. For example, since saccharin is 300 times
sweeter than sugar, it takes much less saccharin to
provide the sweetness of the large mound of sugar.**

Aspartame

The third important substitute sweetener, **aspartame** (now sold under the trade name NutraSweet), was also discovered entirely by accident. In 1965, at the G. D. Searle laboratories, chemists were
preparing compounds to be tested as anti-ulcer drugs. One of the
chemists accidentally tasted some material he got on his finger when
he licked it to pick up a piece of paper. He discovered aspartame's
remarkably sweet taste, and now this substance, as NutraSweet, appears in thousands of foods and drinks.

All of these substances have different degrees of "sweetness."
Saccharin is the sweetest. It is about 300 times as sweet as sucrose
(common table sugar). Cyclamates are about 30 times as sweet as
sucrose and aspartame is about 200 times as sweet.

HOW YOU CAN ...

Test the Sweetness of Artificial Sweeteners

What you need ...

1 packet each of Sweet'n Low, NutraSweet, and table sugar

What you do ...

1. Open one package and touch the white powder with a wet finger.

2. Put your finger in your mouth and taste the sweetener.

3. Rinse off your finger and repeat the test with each of the other two sweeteners.

4. Make an approximate comparison of the relative sweetness of the three sweeteners. Which is the sweetest? Which is the least sweet?

What happened ...

You probably found that the saccharine seemed the sweetest and table sugar the least sweet. Try the same test on your family and see what they think.

THIS DISCOVERY WAS
A STRETCH

Du Pont Chemists Make Nylon

There is a saying that "it is better to be lucky than smart." It may not really be better, but the story of nylon seems to show that it certainly helps.

The story began when Wallace Hume Carothers was brought to the Du Pont chemical company. Carothers started a program aimed at producing synthetic (man-made) materials like the natural substances **cellulose**, silk, and rubber. Although by 1934 his group had contributed valuable knowledge in these areas, Carothers had just about decided that their efforts to produce a synthetic fiber like silk were a failure. Then an accident occurred when his chemists were just "fooling around" in the laboratory. This accident turned the failure into an enormous success that was advertised at the 1939 New York World's Fair as "Nylon, the Synthetic Silk Made from Coal, Air, and Water!"

The basic material that formed nylon (a man-made material called a **polyamide**, having a structure similar to that of silk) had already been made, but it didn't seem to have any useful properties, so it was put aside on the laboratory shelf. Instead, the chemists chose to work on the **polyester** series. These were man-made substances that were softer and dissolved more easily than the polyamide. They were therefore simpler to work with in the laboratory.

**Du Pont chemists discovered nylon when they were
playing games with a new kind of plastic.**

While working with one of these softer materials, chemist Julian
Hill noted that if he gathered a small ball on the end of a glass rod and
stretched it out, it formed a thread that was very silky in appearance.
One day when the boss was downtown, Hill and his fellow chemists
began fooling around with the polyester plastic. They gathered a ball
of the melted material on two stirring rods. One of the chemists took
one of the rods and ran down the hall to see how far he could draw
out the stretched fiber before it broke. They were amazed at how
silky and strong the stretched fiber was.

Although the poly*ester* they used in this way melted too easily to
be used for cloth, they thought of using the poly*amide* that they had
put aside earlier. When they tried the stretching trick with the polyamide, it worked the same way. The fiber became very strong. This is
what the company called nylon. Nylon became the biggest money-
maker the Du Pont company ever had.

This Discovery Was a Stretch

Du Pont began to make women's hose out of nylon. But just when American women were learning how wonderfully strong "nylons" were (they didn't run as often as the old silk stockings), they were taken off the market. This was because nylon was discovered just before World War II and it turned out to be the very best material for making parachutes. American women were even asked to turn in their nylons to be melted down and made into parachutes!

HOW YOU CAN ...

Test the Strength of Nylon

Nylon was especially prized because of its strength. This experiment compares the strength of nylon to that of cotton.

What you need ...

a tree with a sturdy branch

about 6 feet (183 cm) of cotton cord (available at hardware stores)

about 6 feet (183 cm) of nylon seine twine, #18 size (the kind meant for fishing tackle, available at sporting goods stores)

10-pound (4.5-kg) weight (the kind used in pairs on exercise bars would be ideal)

What you do ...

1. Go outside and find a sturdy tree branch that you can reach easily.

2. Tie one end of the cotton cord around the weight, using good, strong knots.

3. Tie the other end of the cotton cord around the tree branch so that the weight hangs about a foot (30 cm) from the ground. (Make sure that there is nothing on the ground underneath the weight that could get hurt if the weight happened to fall.)

4. Hold the weight just below the branch and then drop it. (Be sure not to drop it on your foot!)

5. Repeat steps 2 to 4 using the nylon cord instead of the cotton cord.

What happened ...

The cotton cord probably broke. The nylon cord may have stretched some, but didn't break. Nylon is stronger because the fiber's long polyamide molecules are held together more strongly than the cellulose molecules in cotton.

FROM VELCRO TO
CORN FLAKES

Everyday Life Gets Better Thanks
to Accidental Discoveries

Many things you use every day were discovered by accident. Look around your home sometime and count all the inventions you can find. Whether they were accidental or intentional, think how lucky we are to have them.

Velcro

The hook-and-loop fasteners known by the trade name Velcro are perhaps the best way in the world to connect two things. And like many important discoveries, the idea for Velcro came from an accidental observation.

In the early 1940s, George DeMestral went for a walk in the woods of his native Switzerland. Upon returning home, he noticed that his jacket was covered with cockleburs. (The seeds of the cocklebur plant are spread in nature when the seed burs become attached to passing birds and animals and later drop or are rubbed off.) As DeMestral began picking these burs off, he wondered, "What makes them stick so strongly?"

Notice the hooks on the cocklebur, the inspiration for Velcro.

His curiosity led him to use a magnifying lens to investigate more carefully. He discovered that cockleburs are covered with hooks, and the hooks had become stuck in the loops of the fabric of his cloth jacket, just as they might become attached to the fur of an animal. DeMestral wondered whether something like the cocklebur and the loops of his clothing could be designed that would be useful rather than a nuisance.

The first hook-and-loop Velcro tapes were made in France. (The name "Velcro" comes from the words "*velvet*" and "*crochet*.") Production of the first Velcro tapes was by hand and was very, very slow. Mechanical manufacturing of the loop tape of the fastener was fairly easy, but making the hook part was difficult. The solution was to produce loops that could be cut near the ends to make a hook out of every loop!

Many improvements have been made since the first fasteners were sold. Both the hooks and the loops have been made of better and better materials. First the nylon used to make the hooks and loops was thickened; then the hook was made stronger by blending polyester with the nylon. Pure polyester tape was used to make it

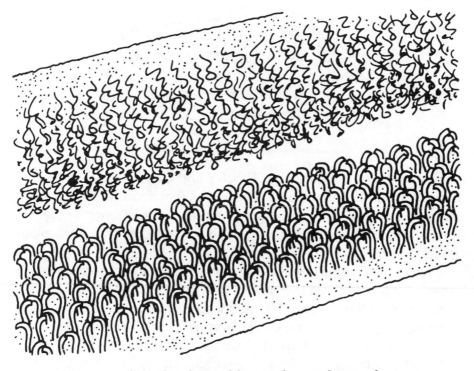

**Close-up of the hooks and loops that make up the two
parts of Velcro.**

resistant to ultraviolet light, chemicals, and moisture. Even steel and
space-age synthetic fabrics are now used to make fasteners that can
withstand temperatures of up to 800°F. These are used in aircraft
and space vehicles.

Many of us have been annoyed by the cockleburs that stick to
our clothing when we walk through the woods. We can all be thankful
to George DeMestral who had the curiosity to find out how it happens and was smart enough to discover how to duplicate this natural
process in such a way as to make our lives more convenient.

Ivory Soap™

Among all the many kinds of soaps, one that is truly different is Ivory
Soap, because it floats! The development of this unusual soap was an
accident. In 1879, an absent-minded worker left a stirring machine
running during the lunch hour and it whipped so much air into the

batch of soap that the makers, Procter and Gamble, at first decided to throw it out. But they hated to waste all that soap, so they made it into bars and sold it. Much to their surprise, they began getting letters from a large number of buyers asking for more of that miraculous "floating soap."

Quick to recognize a sales gimmick, Harley Procter immediately began to advertise that the new floating soap could be used in the bath as well as the laundry. He notched the bars so they could easily be broken in half. He had the soap analyzed to compare it with three popular and expensive imported soaps. When the analysis showed that Ivory Soap contained the fewest impurities, he advertised it as 99 and 44/100 percent pure. And it has been that way ever since.

Corn Flakes and Wheaties®

The process for making corn flakes and Wheaties, two of the most popular breakfast cereals, was discovered by accident. Corn flakes came first, in 1898. The Kellogg brothers (W. K. and J. H.) left some cooked wheat sitting for more than a day before it was run through their rollers. They were surprised and happy to find that it came out flaked instead of in a flat sheet. They tried the same thing with corn, and this gave them corn flakes, which became popular immediately. For some reason, wheat flakes in the form of Wheaties (made by General Mills) did not appear for another 26 years, but now there are many brands of wheat flakes.

Post-its™

Divine inspiration, together with a product failure, gave birth to Post-it self-stick notes, one of the top-selling products of the 1980s.

People who use Post-its today can't imagine what they did without them.

Here's how they were invented. In 1974, Art Fry worked for the 3M Company designing products. On Sundays he sang in a church choir. He marked his choir book with scraps of paper, to make it easier to find the right music quickly. But sometimes the scraps of paper fell out, and Fry had to scramble frantically through the pages. "I don't know if it was a dull sermon or divine inspiration," says Fry, "but my mind began to wander and suddenly I thought of a glue that had been discovered several years earlier by another 3M scientist, Dr. Spencer Silver." Silver had discarded the glue Fry remembered because it was not strong enough to stick permanently. Fry's inspiration was that this glue might serve to keep his place temporarily in the choir book without the paper becoming permanently attached— a "temporarily permanent adhesive," as Fry put it.

When Fry came to work on Monday and began making his bookmarks, it didn't take long before he began to think of other uses for them. He realized it was a good way to make note pads. The idea

was not an instant success, however. The adhesive had to be changed slightly to make it both temporary enough and permanent enough. This took quite a bit of testing.

After nearly a year and a half, Fry was ready to show his sticky notes to the advertising department at 3M. At first these people were not impressed. They were not sure that anyone would pay more for a sticky note pad. In 1977 Post-it notes were sold in four U.S. cities to see how popular they would be. In two of the cities, very few Post-its were sold, but in the other two cities, many people bought them. The 3M Company found out that in the cities where many Post-its were sold, dealers were handing out free samples. People who used them then came back to buy more.

Scotchgard™

Scotchgard fabric protector, 3M's brand of stain repellent, was also an accidental discovery. A chemist spilled a little of a new product on his tennis shoe. Over time, he noticed that the part of the shoe it had spilled on did not get as dirty as the rest of the shoe and he had the sense to think what that might mean. Another accident became a discovery! Now Scotchgard is used on all sorts of fabrics to keep them cleaner longer.

HOW YOU CAN . . .

Test Velcro

What you need . . .

pair of Velcro strips (these can be bought at any fabric shop); you
will need a pair of 1-inch-wide (2½-cm-wide) strips about
2 feet (60 cm) long

magnifying lens

plastic grocery bag

string 10 to 12 inches (25 to 30 cm) long

two 4- or 5-pound (2- or 2.5-kg) sacks of flour

paper punch

What you do . . .

1. Take a strong magnifying lens and look at the two parts of the
    Velcro fastener. Do you see the hooks and loops?

2. To demonstrate the strength of the fastener, do the following:

    a. Tie the loop tape of the Velcro to a door knob or drawer
        handle 3 to 4 feet (90 to 100 cm) from the floor, leaving
        about 4 to 5 inches (10 to 12 cm) of it hanging down.

    b. Place one of the sacks of flour in the grocery bag.

    c. Loop the hook tape of Velcro through the handles of the
        plastic grocery bag with the hooks facing out. Tie the ends of
        the tape together by punching holes in the ends of the
        Velcro tape, pulling a piece of string through the holes, and
        tying the string together.

    d. Attach 3 to 4 inches (8 to 10 cm) of the hook part of the
        Velcro that is tied to the grocery bag onto the loop part of
        the Velcro that is tied to the doorknob.

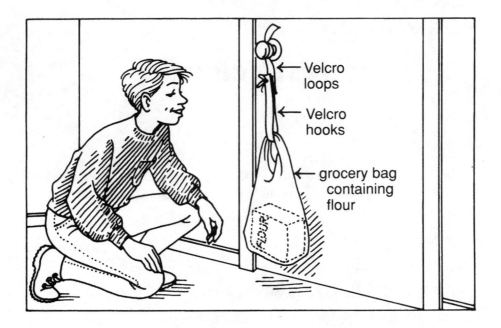

Velcro loops

Velcro hooks

grocery bag containing flour

e. Hold the bag containing the flour just below the doorknob and let it go.

What happened ...

The Velcro pieces remained stuck together and held up the sack containing the flour. Try putting *two* sacks of flour in the plastic grocery bag. Will the Velcro be able to hold up 10 pounds (4.5 kg) in this way?

HOW YOU CAN ...

Test Post-its

Are the original-formula 3M Post-its stronger than other companies' imitations? Let's test them and find out.

What you need ...

1 pad of original 3M Post-its

1 pad of sticky notes made by another company

What you do ...

1. Stick one piece of each kind of note onto the same surface (the edge of a desk or table, or a smooth door).

2. Leave the notes in place for several hours, but look at them from time to time.

What happened ...

One of the notes probably fell off before the other did. Which one stayed stuck on longer? To make the test more scientific, try it five more times on different surfaces. Are the results still the same?

RUBBER THAT RELAXES

Silly Putty™ Becomes a Popular Toy

Silly Putty, first known as "nutty putty," was created during World War II. Scientists were looking for a synthetic rubber for truck and airplane tires, boots, and many other things essential to the war effort because the United States had been cut off from supplies of natural rubber.

In one of the attempts to make synthetic rubber at General Electric Company, chemists used **silicon**, one of the most abundant elements on earth. (Think of how much sand there is in the world—and it is almost half silicon!) The product they came up with was elastic like rubber, but it had other properties that made it less useful. The biggest problem was that it was gooey and would not keep its shape. Imagine a truck tire that quickly became a big, fat, puddle! The people at General Electric thought it still might be good for something, so they sent samples of the material to several scientists and engineers, but no one came up with any good industrial use for it.

In 1949, four years after the war ended, a man named Peter Hodgson, who operated a New Haven toy store, happened to be at a party where the unusual properties of the "nutty putty" were demonstrated. He suddenly had a brilliant idea! He borrowed $147 and

bought as much of the stuff as he could. He paid a Yale student to separate it into 1-ounce (28-gram) balls, packaged these in colored plastic eggs, and named it "Silly Putty."

He advertised the unusual properties of the stuff: it was elastic and bounced beautifully; but when pounded by a hammer, it shattered into many pieces. These pieces could be stuck back together to form a single wad, which slowly flattened out into a puddle. The putty would pick up the printing from a newspaper page, including, especially, the comics; it would remove lint from clothes, animal hair from furniture, and ink from typewriter keys. Popular at first with adults, it soon became a fad with children and, in the 1950s and 1960s, over $6 million of sales per year were recorded.

HOW YOU CAN ...

Discover What Silly Putty Will Do

Get some Silly Putty and try some of the things just mentioned. If you aren't already familiar with this stuff, you will really be surprised.

Try transferring a comic strip character to your Silly Putty.

OUT OF THE BOMB AND INTO THE FRYING PAN

Plunkett Discovers Teflon

Teflon, the billion-dollar product of the Du Pont Company, has a lot of practical uses, from nonstick frying pans to space suits to artificial heart valves. Its discovery resulted from an accident observed by Roy J. Plunkett, a young chemist. On April 6, 1938, Dr. Plunkett decided to open a tank containing a special gas to use in another experiment. But when the tank valve was opened, no gas came out. This was strange, because the weight of the tank indicated that it should be full of the gas.

Instead of just discarding this tank and getting another to continue his research, Plunkett decided to satisfy his curiosity about the "empty" tank. Having first determined that the valve was not faulty by running a wire through its opening, he sawed the tank open and looked inside. There he found a waxy, white powder. As a chemist, he realized what this must mean: the small molecules of the gas had combined with one another many, many times to produce a white solid. No one had ever observed this happening with this particular gas before, but somehow it had happened inside the mysterious "empty" tank.

Plunkett found that the waxy, white powder had remarkable properties. It was more **inert** than sand. That means that it was not affected by strong acids, bases, or heat, and no solvent could dissolve it. However, in contrast to sand, it was extremely slippery. In spite of these unusual properties, it was put on the back shelf.

In a few months, however, scientists involved in creating the first atom bomb needed a material that would resist corrosive gas. The Du Pont company produced Teflon for this use during the war. But the public knew nothing about Teflon until after the war.

It wasn't until 1960 that the first Teflon-coated muffin tins and frying pans appeared on the market. When they were first introduced to the public, these Teflon products were somewhat disappointing. Although the plastic was perfect as a nonstick cooking surface, it was difficult to fasten it securely to metal utensils. It therefore tended to scrape off or peel away from the utensil after repeated washing and scrubbing. After various techniques were tried and four generations of Teflon coatings were produced, Du Pont perfected nonstick pots and pans. Meanwhile, many other uses for Teflon had been discovered.

Roy Plunkett took pride in the many ways that Teflon has touched the lives of millions of people worldwide. He said he "couldn't get over" the letters and calls he received from people who were still alive because of a Teflon heart artery or **pacemaker** (a Teflon-enclosed instrument that keeps the heart beating regularly). Because it is one of the few substances that the body doesn't reject, Teflon can also be used for artificial eye and ear parts; substitute bones for chin, nose, and skull; replacement hip and knee joints, and more.

Teflon has been used for the outer skin of space suits. It is the insulating material for electrical wires and cables that have resisted the violent heat of the sun on the moon. The nose cones and other heat shields and the fuel tanks of space vehicles have been fabricated from Teflon.

All of these remarkable and valuable applications have grown out of the serendipitous discovery by Roy Plunkett. An accident, yes, but a discovery only because of the curiosity and the intelligence of the man to whom the accident occurred.

Teflon is very useful for a wide range of products.

HOW YOU CAN ...

Test Teflon

Teflon is used most often in things that the average person never sees or hears about (heart valves and space ship noses, for example). Probably the only example you've heard of is the coating on frying pans and baking tins.

What you need ...

ordinary frying pan

Teflon-coated frying pan

2 eggs

What you do ...

Ask an adult to fry an egg in each of the two pans, then slide the eggs onto a plate.

What happened ...

The egg easily slipped out of the Teflon-coated pan. The egg cooked in the ordinary pan probably got stuck. The Teflon-coated pan should also be much easier to clean than the other pan.

EPILOGUE

How Accidents Become Discoveries

Remember the definition of the word *serendipity* from the introduction to this book? "Discoveries made by the three princes of Serendip by accident and sagacity of things they were not in quest of." Serendipity has become a popular word to describe "lucky" discoveries. You have probably realized that in *every* example of accidental discovery in this book, the accidents became discoveries only because of the sagacity (intelligence) of the people who encountered the accidents. These people shared several qualities that helped them turn accidents into discoveries. You, too, can develop these qualities in yourself.

The main characteristic shared by many of those who turned accidents into discoveries is *curiosity*. Instead of just ignoring the accident, they were curious to find out more about why it happened or what it meant.

Another characteristic they shared is *perception*. They observed something, recognized that it was important, and took note of it. Undoubtedly many people had seen water run over the edge of a tub or cockleburs sticking to clothing, but they did not discover how to measure the volume of an irregular object or a way to stick almost any two things together. Another scientist, Albert Szent-Gyorgyi, said it well: "Discovery consists of seeing what everybody has seen and thinking what nobody has thought."

Although curiosity and perception may be more natural in some people than in others, these traits can be encouraged and developed. You can train yourself to notice anything unusual and to record your observations, whether you think they are correct or important or not. You should try to be flexible in your thinking and interpretations. The person who sees only what is expected and discards unexpected results as "wrong" will make no discoveries.

Another way in which a person can prepare to benefit from accidents is through careful study in the chosen field of investigation, or *preparation*. Some of the discoveries we have described would not have happened if the investigator had not been prepared to recognize that the accident yielded the hoped-for result, although in a totally unexpected way. For example, Goodyear quickly recognized that the accident of heating rubber with sulfur had the effect of making the elasticity of rubber remain unaffected by heat and cold, something he had been seeking for many years. Because of his preparation, he knew exactly how to test his product.

Consider some of the accidents we have described: an apple falls to the ground at Newton's feet; a boy throws a rock into a dark cave and hears an unexpected sound; a mold spore falls into Fleming's open petri dish; a Du Pont chemist finds that no gas comes out of a tank even though the tank has a weight that shows it is not empty. Any of these accidents could have gone unnoticed. Instead, because of the sagacity of the individuals who encountered the accidents, we have an explanation of the laws that govern the movement of the planets and of our own bodies on this earth; the Dead Sea Scrolls; the "miracle drug" penicillin; and Teflon for frying pans and heart valves.

These are just a few of the benefits of serendipity. Some of these discoveries were made centuries ago, some recently. In the twentieth century, our knowledge in science, medicine, and technology has grown at a fantastic rate. We cannot know what advances the future may bring—interplanetary space travel? A cure for cancer? But we can be sure that accidents will continue to happen and, with human minds better prepared than ever before, we can expect these accidents to be turned into discoveries, marvelous beyond our imagination.

GLOSSARY

amphorae   Ancient Greek pottery jars with two handles, often used to hold wine.

anatomy   The study of the body parts of humans and animals.

antibiotic   A substance made from molds, bacteria, or other living substances that can kill or inhibit the growth of harmful bacteria or other germs. Antibiotics are used to treat diseases.

antibody   A protein produced by the body that creates immunity to a disease.

antiseptic   A substance that kills germs. Antiseptics are usually used to treat external wounds.

archaeologist   Someone who studies past human life, using objects dug from the ground or found on the ocean floor. The objects are usually such things as bones, pottery, tools, and even ancient buildings.

archaeology   The study of past human life, using objects dug from the ground or found on the ocean floor (see **archaeologist**).

aspartame   An artificial sweetener (sold as NutraSweet) discovered in 1965 that is 200 times sweeter than sugar.

astronomer   Someone who studies the stars, planets, and other objects in space.

atom   The smallest part of an *element* that can participate in a chemical reaction.

bacteriology   The study of bacteria.

battery   Usually a group of two or more *cells* connected together, which stores electric charges. Today, some batteries are made of just one cell.

camera obscura   A very simple camera invented over 450 years ago. It was a box with a lens in one end and a glass plate in the other. The image coming through the lens appeared upside-down on the glass plate.

cell (or galvanic cell)   A combination of two different metals, with a material in between (such as wet cardboard). Electric charges flow from one metal to the other through the material in between. Cells are usually combined to make *batteries*.

cellulose   A natural substance occurring in cotton and other plant materials.

collodion   A preparation used in the 1800s as a temporary covering over wounds. It is a jelly-like solution of cellulose nitrate in ether and alcohol. Cellulose nitrate is *cellulose* that has been mixed with nitric acid.

cyclamates   Artificial sweeteners discovered in 1937 that are 30 times sweeter than sugar. They were banned from use in the United States in 1970.

density   A measure of weight per unit of volume.

dielectric   Describes a material that does not allow electricity to pass through.

electric charge   The result of magnetic particles attracting and repelling each other.

electric current   A constant flow of magnetic particles.

electron   A tiny magnetic particle.

electroscope   A scientific instrument used to detect *electric charges*.

electrostatic generator   A machine that produces *electric charges*.

element   A substance composed of only one kind of *atom*.

enzyme   A protein made by a living body and used by the body to slow down or speed up some process in the body. For example, some enzymes in the stomach speed up the process of digesting food.

excavation   Diggings done to uncover objects that might give clues about past life.

fix   In photography, this word means to save an image on a surface (such as a metal plate or photographic paper).

genus   A kind of biological classification of organisms, usually consisting of several species.

gravity   The natural force of attraction that every object has for another object. *Gravity* is often used to mean the attraction of things to the earth.

hieroglyphics   Ancient Egyptian writing that uses pictures for letters.

inert   In chemistry, this describes something that is not easily affected by acids, bases, or heat, and is also hard to dissolve.

inoculation   A method of introducing specially prepared germs into a person's body.

lysozyme   The *enzyme* in a human tear that kills bacteria.

mammoth   A huge, extinct prehistoric mammal related to the present-day elephant, and very similar to the *mastodon*, another prehistoric mammal. The main difference between mammoths and mastodons was the shape of their molar teeth. Both animals had thick fur and tusks that were much longer than elephants' tusks.

mastodon   A huge, extinct prehistoric mammal related to the present-day elephant, and very similar to the *mammoth*.

molecule   The smallest part of a chemical substance that has all of the properties of the substance.

nebula   A group of stars.

pacemaker   A clocklike electrical device, sometimes enclosed in Teflon, that is usually surgically attached to a person's heart to keep it beating regularly.

penicillin   The *antibiotic* substance made from the Penicillium mold. Penicillin kills the bacteria that are responsible for many human illnesses.

phenol   A powerful *antiseptic* that kills certain germs and also kills white blood cells. It is a simple chemical compound sometimes called carbolic acid.

polyamide   A type of chemical compound (that could be either natural or man-made) that includes silk and other compounds similar in structure to silk.

polyester   A type of man-made chemical compound that has been used in making fibers and plastics. Polyesters are softer than *polyamides* and dissolve more easily.

pulsar   The remains of an exploded star. Pulsars make regular bursts of *radiation*, or pulses.

radiation   Energy sent from a source (such as an explosion) through radio waves or light.

saccharin   An artificial sweetener discovered in 1879 that is 300 times sweeter than sugar.

sagacity   Intelligence, especially the ability to perceive things well and make good decisions about them.

serendipity   A discovery that is made by accident and *sagacity*. This means that the person making the discovery has the sagacity, or intelligence, to understand that the accident is showing him or her something new and important.

silicon   One of the most abundant chemical *elements* found on earth. Sand is almost half silicon. Silicon is used to make many electronic devices.

staphylococcus A kind of bacteria that can attack skin and mucous membranes, causing what are often called "staph" infections.

static electricity   The result of many magnetic particles combining to make one big *electric charge*.

sucrose   The chemical name for common table sugar.

synthetic   Man-made.

terrestrial   Relating to the earth.

vaccination   A medical procedure that prevents a person from catching a particular disease. This is done by introducing specially prepared germs into the person's body. Today, a vaccination is usually given by injection (giving a "shot"), or by scratching the germs into the skin with small needles.

vaccine   The specially prepared germs used in a *vaccination*.

voltage   The amount of power stored in a battery.

volume   How much space is taken up by an object.

vulcanization   The process of heating rubber with sulfur to make the rubber less sensitive to temperature changes, so that it remains flexible.

waning   Getting smaller.

waxing   Getting larger.

INDEX